Hal•Leonard
Classical
PLAY-ALONG™

Volume 2

Guiseppe
SAMMARTINI
(1695-1750)

Concerto for Soprano (Descant) Recorder in F Major

The Hal Leonard Classical Play-Along™ series allows you to work through great classical works systematically and at any tempo with accompaniment.

Tracks 2-4 on the CD demonstrate the concert version of each movement. After tuning your instrument to Track 1 you can begin practicing the piece. Using the Amazing Slow-Downer technology included on the CD, you can adjust the recording to any tempo you like without altering the pitch. (Note that when using Amazing Slow-Downer, the CD will stop after each track instead of playing continuously.)

- Track No. ☐ – tuning notes
- Track numbers in circles ◯ – concert version
- Track numbers in diamonds ◆ – play-along version

CONCERT VERSION

Manfredo Zimmerman, Soprano (Descant) Recorder

Telemannisches Collegium Michaelstein

ISBN 978-1-4234-6237-8

HAL•LEONARD®
CORPORATION

7777 W. Bluemound Rd. P.O. Box 13819 Milwaukee, WI 53213

In Australia Contact:
Hal Leonard Australia Pty. Ltd.
4 Lentara Court
Cheltenham, Victoria, 3192 Australia
Email: ausadmin@halleonard.com.au

Visit Hal Leonard Online at
www.halleonard.com

CONCERTO

for Soprano (Descant) Recorder in F Major

I

G. Sammartini (1695 - 1750)

Da Capo al Fine

9 **Siciliano**

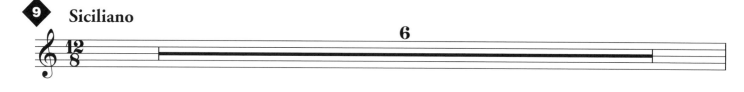